TRAUMA
10 Reasons Why Christians NEED to be Talking About It

Trauma Publishing Unlimited
1944 Brannan Rd.
McDonough, GA 30253
http://www.TraumaEducation.com
© Copyright R. Denice Colson, Ph.D., LPC, MAC, CPCS, CCS, DAAETS.

All rights reserved. You may not reproduce this book in any format, print or electronic, without express written permission from the copyright holders. For further information, email DrColson@TraumaEducation.com. Reviewers may quote brief passages in their reviews.

Disclaimer: Although the author/publisher has made every effort to ensure that the information in this book was correct at press time and while this publication is designed to provide accurate information regarding the subject matter covered, the author/publisher assumes no responsibility for errors, inaccuracies, omissions, or any other inconsistencies herein and hereby disclaim any liability to any party for any loss, damage, or disruption caused by errors or omissions, whether such errors or omissions result from negligence, accident, or any other cause. This publication is meant to be a source of valuable information for the reader; however, it is not a substitute for direct expert assistance. If such a level of assistance is required, you should seek the services of a competent professional.

Dedication

To my parents, Jack and Marty Adcock, who from before my birth saw me as a blessing from God. They believed in me and taught me about Jesus, fed the flame in me, and have always supported and been a part of my adult ministries. I love you both and am so grateful for all you've given me.

Contents

About the Author vii
Regarding the alphabet soup behind her name: ix
Introduction 1
Part One: The 10 Reasons 5
  Reason #1: Christians are affected by trauma. 7
  Reason #2: Pastors and ministry staff are affected by trauma in unique ways. 15
  Reason #3: Childhood trauma is much more common than you think. 21
  Reason #4: Childhood trauma increases the likelihood of adult trauma. 27
  Reason #5: Things we might consider everyday life events can create more post-traumatic stress symptoms than life-threatening events. 31
  Reason #6: Childhood trauma decreases people's lifespan, decreasing opportunities to hear and respond to the Gospel. 37

Reason #7: Childhood trauma negatively affects people's view of God and their ability to form a healthy emotional attachment with God. 39

Reason #8: Childhood trauma negatively affects people's ability to form healthy emotional attachments with other people. .. 43

Reason #9: Childhood trauma is at the root of addiction and mental health issues. 49

Reason #10: The church knows the secret — God heals trauma and uses healing to draw people to him. 55

Part Two: Implementing Trauma-Informed Caring in Your Christian Community 61

Conclusion 87

References 89

About the Author

Denice Colson started her experience in counseling as a senior in high school when her Guidance Counselor invited her to take part in a new peer counseling program. She went to college intending to go to medical school and was on a pre-med track studying biology. However, after discovering her aversion to blood (she nearly passes out), Denice decided to take as many psychology classes as possible. Still, she graduated with a BA in Biology with the equivalent of a minor in psychology. After graduation, she lived and worked at a residential adolescent treatment center in a wilderness setting before attending graduate school at Georgia State University.

Denice earned an MS in Community Counseling in 1985 and, in 2013, completed a Ph.D. in Christian Counseling and Spiritual

Direction at the International University for Graduate Studies, based in Dominica, West Indies. Denice began specializing in trauma recovery in 1992 before it became trendy. In 2013, she abandoned the previous trauma model and felt called to develop a more comprehensive, biblically integrated model. That grew into The Strategic Trauma & Abuse Recovery System: A Christian-Integrated, Comprehensive, 3-Phase Model for Individual and Group Counseling, available on Amazon.com.

Regarding the alphabet soup behind her name:

Ph.D. – (2013) This is Denice's highest-earned degree from the International University for Graduate Studies, based in Dominica, West Indies, accredited by the National Accreditation Board (NAB) of the Commonwealth of Dominica. She also earned an MS in Community Counseling from Georgia State University in 1985.

LPC – Licensed Professional Counselor. Denice received licensing from the state of Georgia in 2002. However, she was first licensed in Texas from 1989 through 2010.

MAC – Master Addiction Counselor. Denice has had this certification through NAADAC, the Association for Addiction Professionals, since 2007. She started working in substance abuse treatment when she began performing trauma work in 1992.

CPCS – Certified Professional Counselor Supervisor (Georgia). She has held this certification since 2016 as the 135th-approved supervisor in Georgia. She was previously certified in Texas as a counselor supervisor in 1996.

CCS – Certified Clinical Supervisor (Georgia) for addiction professionals issued in 2015.

DAAETS – Diplomat status in the American Association of Experts in Traumatic Stress. This award is the second-highest level of achievement in one of the leading organizations focused on trauma and traumatic stress.

Although not represented with initials behind her name, Denice is also a born-again Jesus follower, committed to making Him known. Her mission is to connect wounded people to God's healing grace. God has given her a big vision to see people everywhere breaking the generational cycle of trauma.

Introduction

'M JUST A girl with a passion for introducing people to Jesus. Although I have taken some seminary classes as part of my Ph.D. program, I don't claim to be a theologian. I started my walk with God when I was very young, inviting Jesus into my life when I was probably four or five years old. My relationship with Him continued to grow as I grew. As a youth, I participated in evangelism programs with my family. I prayed with people on the street, in a movie theatre, at their door, in church, and in the schoolyard. In middle school, I prayed with a friend who was new to the school and depressed. Her family had moved from Fiji, and I told her about Jesus. She prayed to accept Him sitting on one of the large planters in the courtyard. I then invited her to church, and she and her parents came the following Sunday. My dad was the pastor, and he could tell her mother wanted to come forward at the end of the service, but her father wouldn't allow it. The following Sunday, however, they all came forward as a family. I can still remember the joy and excitement that we all experienced. I have been told that this started a wave of salvation throughout their extended family, and it also led to a new Christian ministry. Wow! If my friend had never accepted Christ after praying that day in the courtyard, things may not have turned out as they did. It led both of us to a greater understanding of just how awesome God's plan for our lives really is.

The excitement of seeing someone come to believe in Jesus has never left me. As an adult, I have had the opportunity to pray with people while on mission trips and at church. I brought this same spirit of evangelism into counseling. While, traditionally, we associate evangelism with talking, professional counseling is about listening. Initially, I struggled with my need to defend God, and I talked too much. People who have experienced trauma can become so angry at God; they can't see that He is good. Or, if they say they believe

He's good, it's not reflected in their behavior. As a young counselor, I tried to talk people into believing that God is for them. It didn't work. They just felt like I didn't understand them and therefore left counseling. Eventually, I realized God doesn't need me to defend Him. He wants me to represent Him. There is clearly a difference. He needs me to do my job — listen, empathize, comfort, and walk with people through a trauma recovery process. God inspired me and gave me the courage to develop a Christian, Bible-integrated trauma recovery program.

The process includes writing stories about the perpetrator and analyzing its long-term impact. This intensive process changes people's views of God, themselves, and other people. These changes take time, but many people have returned to me after finishing their trauma healing protocol and shared terrific news. They start going to church, praying, and asking questions like, "How do I become a Christian?" One person began attending a Jewish Bible study. Evangelism does not always have to look the same. Counseling doesn't have to be preaching, witnessing, or persuading. We can do our job, and the Holy Spirit can do His. Let's help people heal from the wounds of trauma, and they will more clearly hear the Holy Spirit calling to them!

PART ONE
The 10 Reasons

Reason #1:
Christians are affected by trauma.

While most people won't come right out and say it, there is a pervasive belief that when you put your faith in Jesus Christ, you get a new brain, a new past, and are no longer affected by your past life or childhood. Perhaps this comes from the misinterpretation of 2 Corinthians 5:17, "Therefore, if anyone is in Christ, he is a new creation. The old has passed away; behold, the new has come" (The Holy Bible New Living Translation (NLT), 2004). This passage is actually about reconciliation with God, who reconciled us to Himself through Christ's death and resurrection. It's not about getting a brain transplant.

Or perhaps people think they're supposed to ignore their past adversity or trauma. I've heard this taught in my church. However, it's a misinterpretation of Philippians 3:13-14, in which Paul wrote, "Brothers, I do not consider that I have made it my own. But one thing I do: forgetting what lies behind and straining forward to what lies ahead, I press on toward the goal for the prize of the upward call of God in Christ Jesus" (NLT, 2004). Paul isn't talking about forgetting past trauma or ignoring past life issues but refusing to rely on past accomplishments and law. He's straining toward the prize, total reliance on Jesus for his salvation. Also, in 2 Corinthians 11, Paul lists a lot of the adversity he had experienced, using it to brag about his weakness, demonstrating the point that Christ is strong in our weakness, not in our strength or denial of pain.

Christians are saved through faith in Jesus Christ and called to live an abundant life. However, salvation does not prevent your brain, body, and mind from being affected by past or future traumatic events. As you read this, you might think, "Well, of course not!" Yet many church-attending Christians do not think as deeply about salvation and assume we are offering them a "better life," instant relief from their pain. When they don't get this instant relief, or it's temporary, they give up and turn against God and the church.

Jesus used the parable of the farmer and the different soils to talk about this. This world so hardens some hearts that they can't receive the simple truth about Jesus, and the enemy snatches it away like a bird snatches food. Some souls look good on the surface, believe the truth, and even begin to grow spiritually. But, because there are rocks beneath the surface and weeds and thistles planted simultaneously, they stop growing, wither and die. Jesus' audience was a group of farmers and people who lived off the land. They understood planting and harvesting much more than we do now. Considering what Jesus didn't say, because He didn't have to, no one plants in poor soil on purpose. They try to improve the ground so that the seed has a chance to grow. Jesus acknowledged that not all hearts come to us the same; not everyone is as prepared as others. We may have to help people dig out the rocks and pull up some weeds.

We may not be able to do anything about wealth and privilege, which can create a hard heart, but we can get down on our knees, help dig out rocks and pull up weeds.

Research shows that past trauma, especially trauma experienced in childhood, distorts your view of yourself, God, and others, and not in a positive way. Instead, these experiences create a hardened heart. Jesus didn't promise a trauma-free life. He said, "Here on earth you will have many trials and sorrows. But take heart, because I have overcome the world." (John 16:33, NLT, 2004). This verse doesn't mean we won't have wounds, even from childhood. But Jesus wants to heal us, restore what the trauma stole from our identity, and use those wounds to grow our faith, hope, and love. He wants to take what the enemy meant for evil and use it for spiritual and emotional growth.

There are also a growing number of Christians who believe that bad things won't affect you if you have enough faith. If this were true, then Jesus wouldn't have experienced persecution. People wouldn't have turned against Him even after he raised a man from the dead. Paul wouldn't have had to list his many beatings, stonings, and arrests for his faith in Jesus. These are two of the most faith-filled people who have lived on Earth. And I say, "people," knowing that Jesus was entirely God and entirely man, facing all the temptations we face. Still, He hurt when people rejected Him; He got angry when people didn't believe, and He grieved when they couldn't see the truth.

The Brain and Stress — The Moderator of Trauma

While trauma affects adults and children alike, children are more vulnerable to traumatic experiences and toxic stress levels. It's about our brain, and not about our faith in God. Children's brains are more malleable and easily shaped by their environment. We are born with millions of brain neurons, but they have not been organized yet. Our environment shapes neuropathways and the billions of synapses using "serve and return" behavior. When a baby cries for help, whether from a dirty diaper or hunger, the caretaker's response shapes the baby's expectations. Children treated with gentleness and kindness learn that their environment is safe and can securely reach out for help again. Children who are treated harshly or ignored will learn to stop expressing their needs or expect harsh treatment in the future (Harvard University - Center on the Develop-ing Child, N.D.).

Learning to manage stress is an essential part of development. There are three gen-eral levels of stress: Positive, Tolerable, and Toxic. Positive stress raises the heart rate, increases the release of stress hormones slightly, and is generally the stress you feel getting out of bed, going about your daily business, going out to dinner, etc. Tolerable stress is more severe stress, but it's tempo-rary. Your heart rate and stress hormones increase more. Relationships curb this type of stress, as well as the ability to anticipate it will end. You might feel this kind of stress when giving a presentation at work, driving through traffic, or having a difficult conver-sation with someone.

We experience toxic stress when an event is so stressful that it triggers the brain's fight-or-flight response, causing the heart rate to soar, increases the release of stress hormones, and seems to have no end in sight. Children experience toxic stress when being abandoned, hearing fighting and screaming, name-calling or experiencing physical abuse. Toxic stress triggers the stress response system in their brains, the fight-or-flight response (Harvard University - Center on the Developing Child, N.D.).

To children and adolescents, salvation in Christ offers hope for a new life. Still, many of them return home to these same environments filled with toxic stress. When they don't have a comforting adult to help them through this stressful time, and it continues or is frequent, the "switch" in their brains can get turned on permanently. That means their brains are still in fight-or-flight mode even after the stressful event has ended. Even after becoming adults, the response continues, although the events have ended. Salvation doesn't remove the impact of trauma on the brain and body. Transformation or sanctification, however, is the renewing of our mind. When past trauma is identified, talked about, and grieved, healing becomes part of transformation.

Trauma also affects adults. It's not about a lack of faith, rather our brains aren't immune to toxic stress. While adults can reason, defend themselves, and think through situations, being attacked at knifepoint, robbed, beaten, or raped is still extremely traumatic and requires time to heal and recover. When a loved one dies, we always grieve. Paul wrote that we don't grieve without hope when the loved one is a follower of Christ. Yet, we still suffer.

Take Action

Perhaps we can more directly acknowledge that Christians are affected by trauma. We can encourage people to grieve over personal and corporate events. Clearly state that salvation is about a relationship with God and not a magic eraser. Encourage people to let down their masks and their walls. Maybe they will view transformation as a valuable process and not a destination or a competition.

Reason #2:
Pastors and ministry staff are affected by trauma in unique ways.

Pastors and ministry staff are crisis managers, just like firefighters, police officers, nurses, and doctors. Crisis managers deal with other people's trauma daily. And, like other crisis managers, many pastors are suffering from behavioral health issues, relational issues, and addiction. We've seen multiple suicides, pastors removed because of overt sins like extramarital affairs, pornography addiction, and even child abuse. Research shows that these behaviors are linked to childhood trauma, meaning an increased likelihood that people will get caught up in them if they carry unresolved childhood trauma. People in ministry are redeemed and called, hopefully, in that order, but they are not immune to trauma.

Crisis managers maintain their Professional Identity 24 hours a day, unlike other workers. For example, a server in a restaurant goes home after work and isn't serving everywhere they go. A bank teller leaves the bank and leaves that role behind. Even after leaving their paying job, a police officer, firefighter, or counselor maintains that role. Pastors are pastors 24 hours a day. It is a second identity that they can't leave behind.

Therefore, pastors and ministry leaders have two identities, like other crisis managers. They have a Personal Identity, the one they were born with, and a Professional Identity, which they adopted later. Think of your identity as a piece of fabric with the threads all tightly woven together. The threads represent values, beliefs, expectations, views of others, life, and God. Pastors have two pieces of fabric. Their personal values and beliefs, along with a calling from God, led them into their career. They trained for ministry, not just teaching God's Word but managing staff and congregation, so they adopted the new, Professional Identity. Their seminary or bible college taught them to expect disasters, deaths, and possibly counsel a deacon having an affair. Personally, however, these situations contradict their values, beliefs, and expectations. These contradictions break the threads of their identity, creating losses and grief.

The problem comes when the Professional Identity absorbs the traumatic event, like the death of a parishioner's child, but the Personal Identity is wounded. The wound is complicated when the Professional Identity denies that the Personal Identity is injured. When the pastor/minister refuses to address the damage to their Personal Identity through talking, grieving openly, counseling, or other means, it festers, spreads, and eventually impacts the Professional Identity. Pastors, like counselors, take an oath of confidentiality and may use that as a reason not to talk about it. But the loss and grief don't just go away. They get buried in the memory system of the brain and continue to impact conscious decisions and behavior. These crisis managers will start changing their behavior, and these changes affect the people around them. At first, it may be a slight emotional withdrawal from their spouse, family, or friends. Emotional withdrawal creates more loss, however, and a snowball effect ensues. Over time, this can lead to overworking, divorce, and even affairs.

Studies by Fuller Institute, George Barna, and Pastoral Care, Inc. show that:

- 1,500 clergy leave the pastoral ministry each month.
- 83% of clergy spouses want their spouses to leave the pastoral ministry (Hartford Institute for Religious Research).
- 90% of clergy in all denominations will not stay in ministry long enough to reach retirement age (U.S. Bureau of Labor and Statistics).
- 50% of pastors indicate they would leave the ministry if they had another way of making a living (Hartford Institute for Religious Research).
- 80% believe pastoral ministry has negatively affected their families. Many pastor's children do not attend church now because of what the church has done to their parents.
- 33% state that being in the ministry is an outright hazard to their family.

- 75% report significant stress-related crises at least once in their ministry.
- 90% feel inadequately trained to cope with the ministry demands.
- 33% confess having been involved in inappropriate sexual behavior with someone in the church.
- 11% (1 in 9 pastors) admitted committing adultery (Retrieved from ShepherdsWatchmen.com)

I don't list these statistics to say how bad pastors are; it's quite the opposite. People are called into ministry with high ideals and high hopes. Like police officers and firefighters, they are there for people during their worst moments, but spend more time taking care of others than of themselves, and by extension, their families. They are much more vulnerable than the average person because of these ideals and because people put them on a pedestal, forgetting that they're just people too.

Take Action

Perhaps pastors need a type of trauma counseling unique to crisis managers. Most pastors know they aren't in it alone, but many get trapped in the shame of not accomplishing their very lofty goals. Religious associations can normalize trauma for pastors and ministry leaders and offer counseling and intervention for both pastors and their families. Ministry leaders, pastors, deacons, and elders should NOT ignore minor relational problems because they can grow into bigger ones. Proactive counseling could be offered to pastors rather than waiting for problems to appear. Demanding that people take part in counseling rarely works. However, making it available as part of their job description, removing the stigma and providing the pastor or ministry leader the time and funds to take part in privacy will go a long way for many families.

Reason #3:
Childhood trauma is much more common than you think.

A RESEARCH STUDY FROM 1995 and 1997, called the Adverse Childhood Experiences Study ("ACE"), is significant. The researchers recruited over 17,300 participants through Kaiser Permanente in San Diego, California. These were all middle-class adults, racially diverse, mostly college educated, who had insurance through Kaiser. The ACE Study is a longitudinal project, meaning the participants are still being followed and generating outcomes. The epidemiologist initiating the study, Dr. Vincent Felitti, says the number of people affected by childhood trauma/adversity astonished him. Researchers considered ten types of childhood adversity, including physical abuse or neglect by parents, emotional abuse or neglect by parents, loss of a biological parent to divorce, sexual abuse by anyone, a family member with mental health issues, a family member with substance use issues, a family member going to prison, and domestic violence by father (or stepfather) against mother (or stepmother). Of course, there are many more types of adversity possible, but for research purposes, they narrowed it to these 10 (Felitti et al., 1998). Researchers found that:

- 2/3 of people had at least 1 ACE;
- of those, 1 out of 14 had an ACE score of 4 or more;
- one out of 11 had an ACE score of 6 or more; and
- women were 50% more likely than men to have an ACE score of 5 or more (Center for Disease Control [CDC], 2021).

These outcomes were shocking to the researchers, but other researchers have duplicated the study in various U.S. states and other countries with the same results. These statistics should be appalling to us. Christians, this is awful, and we must be on the front lines of fighting against childhood trauma!

Suppose we apply this to our congregations, small groups, life groups, Sunday School classes, or other Christian organizations. In that case, that means two out of three people have experienced at least one form of childhood adversity. In Christian schools, two out of three children are experiencing something right now! I talked about toxic stress earlier, and childhood adversity causes this level of stress. That means that two-thirds of our group, at any given time, may be in fight or flight. What impact does this have on a leader's attempt to disciple, build unity, encourage participants to share and socialize, or provide support for one another? Is it possible that the lasting shame of childhood abuse, divorce, poverty, or another source of trauma keeps people separate from each other? Are people afraid of what others might think and therefore staying on the outskirts of the church? This is something to contemplate.

I do a lot of speaking about ACEs and have full-day workshops on their impact. There is too much information to list in this small book, but there is a lot more material on ACES in my PowerPoint presentations available at http://SlideShare.net/DeniceColson.

Take Action

Begin to talk to adults about childhood trauma. Normalize it, not as something that's okay to do, but that it's okay if it happened to you. It's happened to many people. Maybe we can ease some of the shame. Perhaps people will talk to each other more spontaneously, join together in their grief, and begin resolving past trauma naturally. We can stop keeping the secret of childhood trauma, bring it into the light, and let the Holy Spirit work.

Many churches have been afraid to interfere with the family system by addressing child abuse and neglect when dealing with children. When I started working as a Master's degree counselor in a church, they didn't want to report suspected child abuse for fear of offending the adults or being sued. This still happens, even when the evidence is pretty strong. The government system is not perfect, and people get angry, especially when they are guilty. There are terrible stories of people wrongfully accused. However, children need protection, and if the church rises to help prevent childhood adversity, less reporting will be required. Perpetrators will avoid churches, rather than seeking them out to gain access to children. Consider offering a workshop from Stewards of Children-Darkness to Light®.

Reason #4:
Childhood trauma increases the likelihood of adult trauma.

THE ACE STUDY researchers created a chart to illustrate the connections between childhood trauma and adult physical, social, relational, and psychological issues. They call it the ACE Pyramid.

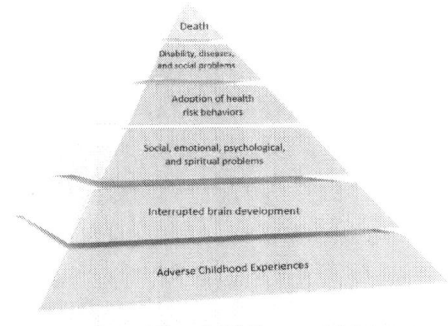

The ACE Pyramid

The pyramid design reflects the research, which shows that not everyone is destined to experience the adverse outcomes that others experience. Researchers believe that "resiliency factors" prevent or preclude some people from moving up the pyramid (Poole, Dobson, & Pusch, 2017). These include, but are not limited to, participation in church, having a youth leader who shows a healthy interest in you, and having a view of God as a friend and loving father.

Research shows that boys and girls who grow up with domestic violence are much more likely to experience or perpetrate domestic violence as an adult. Boys who experience or witness violence are 1,000 times more likely to commit violence than those who do not (van der Kolk, 1998). Boys who are sexually abused are much more likely to impregnate a teenage girl. The higher the ACE score, the more likely a woman will have an unintended pregnancy and elective abortion. The higher the number of ACEs, the more likely the adult will have 50 or more sexual partners, increasing the risk for unwanted pregnancy, socially transmitted diseases, and HIV/AIDs (Anda et al., 2006). After one of my presentations on the ACE study, a woman approached me and shared that she already had over 100 sexual partners, and she was only in her forties. Childhood trauma that goes unaddressed and unresolved creates unhealed emotional and spiritual wounds, which perpetuate more trauma. This trauma occurs in churches too. I have treated many people abused by church and Christian school staff.

Take Action

Helping volunteers deal with their past trauma creates compassion and empathy for the teens and children they work with, decreasing the likelihood of perpetuating trauma with the folks under their care. Perhaps hiring TraumaEducation.com to present a short two hour training on the impact of childhood trauma or using a canned program like Stewards of Children-Darkness to Light®. The information in my book, Break EVERY Stinking Chain! Healing for Hidden Wounds can be used in a small group, a class, or used in a sermon series.

Reason #5:
Things we might consider everyday life events can create more post-traumatic stress symptoms than life-threatening events.

CHILDHOOD TRAUMA HAS more influence on the brain because, as children, our brains are more malleable. We are also more vulnerable to the world around us. However, adult-onset trauma is also destructive and feeds us negative images of God and His people. For example, following an outbreak of foot and mouth disease among livestock in the Netherlands in 2001, nearly 50% of the farmers required to put down livestock showed symptoms of post-traumatic stress at such significant levels they needed professional help (Olff et al., 2005). In other studies, events considered as everyday life events, such as relationship discord, non-sudden death of a loved one, chronic illness, or problems with work or school, generated more Post-Traumatic Stress Disorder (PTSD) symptoms in adults than events considered life-threatening, such as accidents or disasters (Mol et al., 2005, Scott and Stradling, 1994).

While churches commonly recognize the loss of a loved one by offering grief-centered programs, they typically see relationship discord or problems with work and school as weakness or even a lack of faith. This discourages people from talking about it or sharing their pain and loss, causing more damage to their identity, distance between them and the church and sometimes them and God. We overlook other types of losses that we may think of as no big deal when they are a big deal to the person experiencing them.

Let's look at the definition of trauma, at least the one I've developed. "Trauma is any event from outside of your power/control/conscious choice which contradicts your identity, to the point it raises your stress to toxic levels and creates unacceptable losses" (Colson, 2012). Trauma is a wound to your identity. It's not determined by the event, but by the personal experience of the event. What is experienced as traumatic by one person may not be experienced as traumatic by another person, and vice versa. Because there are some universal needs, however, there are some events universally experienced as traumatic. However, research shows "trauma" is not limited to only these events.

Some people say it this way; there's big "T" trauma and little "t" trauma. But, is little "t" trauma less painful and less damaging than big "T" trauma? Years ago, I was visiting a church member in the hospital because she had a heart problem. As I was leaving, I had a sharp pain in my right side and thought, "Hmm, maybe I should step into the ER while I'm here." But the pain stopped, and I headed home. I was in downtown Atlanta and lived 40 minutes out into the suburbs and by the time I got home, the pain was excruciating. My husband drove me to the hospital, as I writhed in pain and tried not to scream. We had three little girls, and they were in the back, terrified. I tried to stay quiet, but I'd never had pain quite like this before, not even in childbirth! The admissions clerk decided I probably had a kidney stone, since I wasn't running a fever, and made me wait. My entire family came, having driven 45 minutes, to stay with me. The only comfortable position I could find was lying on the dirty floor, curled up in a ball, moaning. People were coming up to me, praying for me and saying, "Ma'am, I hope they get to you soon."

I was so disruptive, from crying out in pain, that after three or four hours, they put me in a private waiting room with my husband. Fortunately, someone had taken my children home by then. Six hours passed before they finally took me back and gave me an IV with pain medicine. It turned out I was allergic to the pain medicine they gave me; it made me feel like my body was on fire! I came up off the table screaming, "Get that out of me! What did you give me?" Eventually, I had an MRI, and yes, it was a kidney stone. So, they sent me home with a different pain medicine to wait for it to pass. It took almost two weeks, but eventually, it passed. I was so disappointed. I thought I would pass a baseball, but no, it was a tiny little rock with points all over it like a mace. It was so small that if I threw it at you, you wouldn't even know it had hit you. But inside of me, it was excruciating. With trauma, it's not the size. It's the location.

Take Action

We can give people permission to feel pain and suffer even if we think it's a little thing. Empathize with people and encourage them to tell their stories. You can encourage people to grieve and not minimize their pain. Don't say anything like, "It's not that big of a deal," or "You'll get over it" or "Just get over it and move on." Since it's not inside of you, you don't know how it feels. Nor do you know how this event could affect the rest of their lives. A former client had become an opioid addict, and she almost died. After she got out of rehab and was sober, I worked with her to figure out a source of childhood trauma. She claimed she didn't have any initially, but finally, we came upon it. It was one incident in school where a teacher had inappropriately reprimanded her. This brief event started a snowball of inner pain, shame, and fear. She didn't tell anyone and eventually started using drugs to cope. From the outside, you might think she should have just blown it off.

But to her, it was a life-changing event that caused her more and more pain for years.

Reason #6:
Childhood trauma decreases people's lifespan, decreasing opportunities to hear and respond to the Gospel.

Researchers link an ACE score of six or more to a 20-year decrease in lifespan (Anda et al., 2009). While generally, people are living longer, people with higher ACE scores die earlier. Some of this is because of choices made to manage childhood trauma, like drug and alcohol use, smoking, and other risky behaviors. But there's also evidence that the toxic stress created by childhood trauma affects the body systems directly. Diseases like diabetes and ischemic heart disease are also directly linked to ACEs (Dong et al., 2004; Dube et al., 2003). These diseases decrease people's quality of life, as well as quantity. God wants everyone to hear the Gospel message. While most people who accept Christ do so in childhood, some don't until they are senior citizens. Helping people prolong their lives gives them more time to choose God, serve, and grow His kingdom on Earth.

Take Action

Talk about the impact of childhood trauma and encourage others to talk about it. Encourage parents to learn about trauma, deal with their own trauma, and help them empathize with their children.

Reason #7:
Childhood trauma negatively affects people's view of God and their ability to form a healthy emotional attachment with God.

RESEARCH SHOWS THAT childhood trauma negatively impacts an adolescent/adult survivor's view of God. Some outcomes of various research projects include:

- A lack of worthiness.
- Existential questions about the meaning and purpose of life.
- Unresolved religious questions about the beliefs people grew up with.
- Disillusionment about their faith or religious beliefs.
- Distrust of God.
- Anger at God.

- Chronic guilt, even when accepting God's forgiveness.
- A negative concept of God, especially God being distant, controlling, and mean (Reinert and Edwards, 2009).
- Insecure attachment to God (Reinert and Edwards, 2009).
- Dismissal of God.
- And other miscellaneous spiritual obstacles.

Psychological distress, such as depression or anxiety, is the BEST independent predictor of negative feelings towards God (Eurelings-Bontekoe, Hekman-Van Steeg, & Verschuur, 2005). One's image of God grows out of one's paternal and maternal caregiving images (Brokaw & Edwards, 1994). Parents have the most substantial influence on their adolescent's religiosity (Benson, Donahue, and Erickson, 1989). Therefore, if parents are perpetrators of trauma, as shown in the ACE study, adolescents project this onto God, creating distrust, insecurity, and lack of value. Consequently, poor attachment bonds with God are related to difficulty finding meaning and purpose in life (Beck and McDonald, 2004).

Famous psychologist and psychotherapist, Albert Ellis, was an atheist and very anti-Christian. He taught that religion, especially Christianity, was at the root of most mental health problems. Prior to his death, he had to change his view because of his research. He wrote, "Although I have, in the past, taken a negative attitude toward religion, and especially toward people who devoutly hold religious views, I now see that absolutistic religious views can sometimes lead to emotionally healthy behavior. Research shows that positive health outcomes are associated with a positive view of God as a friend or a loving father. As several studies have shown (Batson et al., 1993; Donahue, 1985; Gorsuch, 1988; Hood et al., 1996; Kirkpatrick, 1997; Larson & Larson, 1994), people who view God as a warm, caring, and lovable friend, and who see their religion as supportive are more likely to have positive outcomes than those who take a negative view of God and their religion" (2000).

Directly addressing trauma helps separate the traumatic events from God and lay them at the feet of the perpetrator, where they belong. This allows the survivor to be more open to positive views of God, seeing Him as safe and for them, not against them. Resolution of traumatic loss allows biblical teaching and discipleship to be more effective. Even evangelism is more effective following trauma recovery. People don't have to be saved to address and heal from trauma, although getting through it is harder without God's hand to hold. When the church reaches out to trauma survivors, accepting them where they are, not trying to change their negative behavior but addressing the trauma wound first, they are more open to believing in a God who loves them and heals their wounds. Then, God can change them and convict them of sinful behaviors.

Take Action

Ask people how they view God and what events they have experienced that have shaped that view. Don't discount past trauma and its impact on both salvation and spiritual growth.

Reason #8:
Childhood trauma negatively affects people's ability to form healthy emotional attachments with other people.

There's even more documentation on how childhood trauma affects an adolescent or adult survivor in the area of relationships. The Adverse Childhood Experiences Study has shown that ACEs are connected in a strong and graded fashion (meaning the more experiences, the more likely these issues will develop) to the following social/relational problems (CDC, 2021):

- Divorce;
- Homelessness;
- Prostitution;
- 50+ sexual partners;

- Delinquency, violence, and criminal behavior;
- Inability to sustain employment;
- Re-victimization by rape;
- Domestic violence, bullying, etc.;
- Compromised ability to parent;
- Teen and unwanted pregnancy;
- Intergenerational transmission of abuse;
- Impaired work performance/missing days of work.

All issues on this list will not be addressed, but I would like to offer some suggestions and insight on a few topics.

Divorce, Domestic Violence, Teen Pregnancy, and Sexual Activity

Divorce is considered an adverse childhood experience which perpetuates trauma and passes it down to the next generation. Divorce is frequently a source of trauma for children, although sometimes, if domestic violence or sexual abuse has been present, divorce can end those traumatic experiences. Childhood adversity increases the likelihood that people will end up divorced as adults.

In general, both marriage and divorce are trending downward. In 2019, for every 1000 marriages, only 14.9 ended in divorce, and this is the lowest rate of divorce in 50 years. However, fewer people are getting married and choosing cohabitation, instead, to solve the divorce problem. When these relationships end, they aren't counted in the divorce statistics. For every 1,000 unmarried adults in 2019, only 33 got married. This number was 35 a decade ago in 2010 and 86 in 1970 (Institute for Family Studies, 2021).

While it is not true that divorce amongst Christians is higher than the general population, it's not much different, and it's still too high. Many Christian couples decide that divorce is a sin and stay married, even though they are miserable, suffer from physical or emotional abuse, or live separate lives in an "open marriage." Many Christians seem to opt for quantity over quality, assuming that staying in an abusive or loveless marriage is better for children. Unfortunately, these types of relationships are just as traumatic for children as divorce; they are sometimes worse.

Boys and girls who witness domestic violence are at increased risk for perpetrating domestic violence as adults. Girls who see their mothers being abused, whether physical or verbal, are at increased risk for teen pregnancy. Elective abortion is linked to childhood adversity, along with the likelihood of an adult having 50+ sexual partners.

As you can see, there is a snowball effect. One choice to use any of these responses to survive trauma can lead to more trauma.

Take Action

Churches are in the perfect position to talk about trauma and help reduce many of these social issues by offering varying types of discipleship classes focused on living out the Gospel. Many churches provide marriage classes, and some offer marriage mentoring. These are great programs and help save many marriages, preventing additional trauma for children and adults. However, these focus on the symptoms rather than getting to the heart of the problem, emotional attachment. Couples struggle with emotional attachment due to childhood attachment wounds. Some of these wounds rise to the level of trauma; some don't. You cannot discount an event because of its size. Massive symptoms can result from single events that people minimize. Every event of trauma, by my definition, counts. Adding the additional focus on past trauma wounds could increase the success of these programs and save even more families from ruin. You might consider another curriculum that focuses on emotional attachment rather than on symptoms found at HowWeLove.com.

In addition, while sin is always a problem, helping people get to the root of their chronic sinful behavior is a great way to help them start thinking about the root and not just the fruit. This isn't a theological discussion, so don't get distracted by inborn sin versus sins we commit daily. People are trapped in these behaviors because they try to manage their buried pain from emotional and psychological wounds. They chose sinful behaviors to survive, yet just choosing behaviors that aren't sinful still doesn't deal with the root, which is unhealed trauma wounds. We can leverage people's broken behavior to help them become more aware of past wounds and God's desire to heal and transform.

Reason #9:
Childhood trauma is at the root of addiction and mental health issues.

DRUG AND ALCOHOL abuse and addiction are rampant in our societies. In 2020, in the U.S., 93,000 people died of drug overdose (CDC, 2021). The ACE study (Felitti, 2004) shows that:

- An ACE score of 5 or more leads to a 500% increase in the likelihood of adult alcoholism, and
- 2/3 of all cases of alcoholism can be attributed to adverse childhood experiences.
- A child with six or more categories of adverse childhood experiences is 250% more likely to become an adult smoker.
- A male child with an ACE score of 6

has a 4,600% increase in the likelihood that he will become an IV drug user later in life.
- An ACE score of 4 or more is linked to severe obesity, a BMI of 35 or more.
- 78% of IV drug abuse and 50% of all types of drug abuse are attributable to ACEs.

The church has made great inroads in helping people recover from substance abuse but could do even more by addressing the root problem of childhood trauma wounds while assisting people in getting sober.

Mental health is deteriorating at an alarming rate. According to the National Institute of Mental Health and Mental Health America:

- 1 in 5 adults struggles with a mental health condition.
- 43.4 million Americans (approx. 1 in 10) struggle with mental health problems yearly.
- 10.4 million of those struggle with serious mental illness.
- 20.2 million adults in the U.S. have experienced a substance use disorder.

- The estimated number of adults with serious suicidal thoughts equals 9.6 million individuals.
- 11.93% of youth (age 12-17) report suffering from at least one major depressive episode in the past year.
- 8.2% of youth (1.9 million) experienced severe depression.
- Rates of youth with severe depression increased from 5.9% in 2012 to 8.2% in 2015.
- 5.13% of youth in America report having a substance use or alcohol problem.
- 3.3 million youth reported the use of marijuana, cocaine, and/or heroin.

Suicide is a mental health crisis (CDC).

- Suicide is the 10th leading cause of death in the U.S., the 3rd leading cause of death for people aged 10–14 and the 2nd leading cause of death for people aged 15-24.
- Suicide rates have increased over 30% in half of the states in the U.S. since 1999.
- According to the Center for Disease

and Control (CDC), nearly 45,000 people committed suicide in 2016, about one death every 12 minutes.
- Daily, an estimated 18-22 veterans die by suicide.
- The estimated number of adults with serious suicidal thoughts is 9.8 million individuals.
- Over 90% of children who die by suicide have a mental health condition.

Mental health issues aren't just an American problem. According to a 2016 study from Our World in Data:

- 1.1 billion people worldwide are struggling with a mental health or substance abuse disorder (about 1 in 6 people); and
- The majority of those struggle with
  - Anxiety (275 million) and
  - Depression (268 million).

According to multiple studies, including the ACE study, depression is linked to childhood trauma. This link has been demonstrated in 251 studies, using a total of 159,793 subjects, conducted by multiple and independent researchers, using different study designs and methods on diverse samples of people (Whitfield, The Truth about Depression, 2003). The ACE study demonstrates that:

- Adults with an ACE score of 4 or more were 460% more likely to be suffering from depression.
- The likelihood of adult suicide attempts increased 30-fold, or 3,000%, with an ACE score of 7 or more.
- Childhood and adolescent suicide attempts increased 51-fold or 5,100%, with an ACE score of 7 or more (Felitti et al, 1998).

One study showed that 51-98% of public mental health clients with severe mental health diagnoses had unaddressed childhood sexual/physical abuse. The same studies showed that 93% of psychiatrically hospitalized adolescents had histories of physical and sexual or emotional trauma in childhood or even more recently (Goodman et al., 1999, Mueser et al., 1998; Cusack et al., 2003).

Statistics link addiction and mental

health issues to past trauma, especially in childhood. The mental health field is coming around to this, but for the most part, it still focuses on symptoms and refuses to address the spiritual issues that result from having a traumatic childhood history. The church could be on the cutting edge, on the front line of providing comfort, relief, and hope to hurting people.

Take Action

Churches can offer classes or support groups for people struggling with addiction and mental health issues. One possibility is using my book, *Break EVERY Stinking Chain!: Healing for Hidden Wounds*, as a small group bible study or a 14-15-week small group program.

Reason #10:
The church knows the secret — God heals trauma and uses healing to draw people to him.

All the points we've covered so far are negative, demonstrating the destructive consequences of sin in people's lives. It is not just their sin, but the sin of others and how it impacts children, family, community, and the world. But if the Christian church has the solution to the world's problems, if Jesus Christ is the answer to the hopelessness and pain in the world, we must do whatever we can to help people hear His message.

Pain is one of the primary motivators for people to seek help and turn to God. In his book, *The Problem of Pain*, C. S. Lewis writes, "God whispers to us in our pleasures, speaks in our consciences, but shouts in our pains. It is his megaphone to rouse a deaf world (1940)." In 2014, LifeWay conducted a study on mental health in the church. Over the spring and summer, they used telephone and online surveys of protestant adults in three groups: pastors, people with acute mental illness, and family members of people with acute mental illness. They defined acute mental illness as "moderate depression, severe depression, bipolar disorder, or schizophrenia." They also interviewed 15 Christian clinical experts about mental illness, how it affects their patients and how churches can better minister to those struggling with mental illness. Results showed that 66% of pastors speak to the church in sermons or large group messages about mental illness either once a year, rarely, or never. 26% of pastors talk about mental illness several times a year, 4% about once a month, and only 3% several times a month.

Take Action

If two-thirds of your congregation is affected by at least one ACE, it's time to acknowledge it openly and begin to normalize the impact. It's naïve to think that your community isn't affected by trauma or mental health issues. It's not a matter of ethnicity, socioeconomic status, or education level. EVERYONE is affected, including those with a strong faith in God.

Several years ago, my sweet 80-year-old mother came to me and said, "I've kept a secret, even from your dad, for all my life. I was raped by my cousin when I was 11 years old." She cried and realized that this experience had changed how she looked at other women who reported abuse. All those years, while she had been worshiping and serving God as a pastor's wife, a Bible teacher, a worship leader, and a disciple-maker, she was suffering from this secret and the shame it caused.

The enemy used this in her life to cause her so much pain. What finally brought her forward was the "Me Too" movement. She didn't understand why so many people were coming forward with their stories and approached a counselor friend about it. The friend told her that these secrets had to come out. They must be verbalized so we can heal. That friend's affirmation gave my mom the courage to share her story. It's never too late, as long as you are breathing!

Church, it's time to step up! The world has become aware that trauma is a real problem, but they only have band-aids, not long-term solutions. We can't rely on the "Me Too" movement and other secular social movements designed to divide and not heal. We must be a force for healing and unity.

When integrated with biblical teaching, psychology and counseling can be highly effective in alleviating symptoms of depression, anxiety, and hopelessness. However, even healthy people have to die someday. As ambassadors for Christ, we offer people not just an abundant life on Earth, but to have an eternity full of boundless joy and happiness with God. But we need to help people where they are now, in their suffering on Earth, not just give them a promise of eternal life after death. People will put off thought about the future for immediate pain relief right now through drugs, alcohol, sex, and other temporary fixes. God wants to heal people's wounds NOW in a way that ensures they won't need those things anymore. As Christians, we can be a part of that by adopting trauma-informed systems and programs in the church.

One of those programs you can adopt is The Strategic Trauma & Abuse Recovery System: A Christian-Integrated, Comprehensive, 3-Phase Model for Individual and Group Counseling, available on Amazon.com. Our goals are to Educate–Empower–Equip.

Break EVERY Stinking Chain!: Healing for Hidden Wounds is the first book and workbook in the series. (Break EVERY Stinking Chain!: Healing for Hidden Wounds, also available on Amazon.com) Counselors, professional and pastoral, can get trained and certified in the treatment model to work with both groups and individuals. For more information, visit http://www.TraumaEducation.com

PART TWO

Implementing Trauma-Informed Caring in your Christian Community

Now that we've discussed the ten reasons, most people ask, "What can I do about it?" and "Where do I start?" You may be in a church, a small group, or a school and want to implement what you've learned. You may be a pastor, a teacher of adults or children, or a serving elder. There are different things people can do, based on their position and their level of influence.

When I finished my MS in 1985, I attended one of the first workshops on adult survivors of sexual abuse hosted by the Georgia Council on Child Abuse around 1986. At that time, they were keeping statistics on women, not men. Their advice was to treat the symptoms and not to have the survivor talk about the trauma. Their thinking was that it re-traumatized the client. When the client cried and grieved, they didn't know what to do and decided it was terrible. Trauma treatment has come a long way since then. Directly talking about trauma is relatively new in the professional counseling arena.

In 1994, Substance Abuse Mental Health Services Administration (SAMHSA) held its first summit on childhood trauma. Since then, the professional counseling world has slowly moved toward recognizing and treating childhood trauma openly and directly. When I first started holding workshops and making presentations, I was frequently challenged and even mocked, laughed at, and harassed for saying there was a link between adult addiction and childhood trauma. With the ACE Study's information, there is more acceptance that trauma is linked to addiction and mental health issues, but that doesn't mean that all counselors agree on how it should be treated or addressed.

Now, trauma-informed care is the minimum requirement expected in behavioral health care. I believe it should also be the minimum in churches and the Christian community. I teach my workshop attendees that there are four levels of development in trauma care for counselors. In my opinion, pastors and churches can also adopt these levels.

Level 1

At this first level, a person realizes and accepts the widespread impact of trauma. Childhood trauma may not be new to our generation, and it may be less common than in previous centuries. However, it is still pervasive and crosses all socioeconomic boundaries. More importantly, people are more willing to talk about it now than ever before.

Level 2

You can now move to recognizing and acknowledging the signs and symptoms of trauma in yourself, staff, parishioners, students, or class members. This level requires making an internal shift from "what's wrong with you?" to "what happened to you?" It means changing the lens through which you view those under your care. Focus on the source of their pain rather than the sinful way they are trying to cope. Jesus did this when He spoke to the woman at the well.

He didn't start the conversation by saying, "Hey, what's wrong with you? You've been married multiple times, and now you're living with a man who isn't your husband. You need to straighten up!" He started with vulnerability, asking her for a favor and showing that He recognized her as a person. His purpose was, of course, to reveal Himself to her and establish Himself as the Messiah. Our purpose is different, but ultimately the same. We want people to know who Jesus is and accept Him and allow Him to heal them. We are all sinners, every single one of us. Our job is not to judge the world but to be ambassadors for Christ. We are to attract people to Him by demonstrating His love, acceptance, truth, and compassion.

Level 3

It is crucial to avoid re-traumatizing people by instituting policies that promote six key principles of trauma-informed care. Applying these in a congregational, small group, or school setting is different from using them in a hospital or counseling center. However, these are all based on biblical principles, and the church can lead the way in demonstrating their use. I've included possible action steps with each one.

Key Principle 1: Safety

To be successful, you must first create an environment that is safe both physically and psychologically. It doesn't mean that people shouldn't feel challenged or that people will never feel uncomfortable. That's impossible and is not helpful. Growth requires discomfort and sometimes pain. It means you go out of your way to make people feel welcome, provide for their needs, and don't create a hostile environment, no matter their appearance. Clients have mentioned one issue in the past: the "greeting time," when people shake hands and hug. Some people don't want others touching them because of past childhood abuse. The pandemic of 2020 has taken care of this, for now. However, not having any designated greeting time can leave people feeling isolated and ignored. So, finding a balance is necessary for each congregation. Perhaps everyone turns and waves at each other? It's a difficult situation, but one we can discuss from the perspective of a trauma-informed lens.

Small groups, bible studies, and schools can apply this in other ways. Small groups can be tricky because trauma survivors tend to go to extremes. They may be highly withdrawn or dominating in their conversation. They may be overly sensitive and easily offended, or insensitive and offending in their speech. Creating a safe environment for everyone means setting boundaries with some and giving special attention to others. Looking beyond the behavior and asking yourself, "What's happened to this person to bring them to this point?" is a strategy that can help build cohesion in the group and feed each person's sense of safety.

Of course, no matter what you do, some people will not feel safe. They will also blame you as a leader. Be intentional and do your best for each person while not neglecting the others in your group. Keep in mind that your goal is creating a safe environment that is also challenging, uncomfortable and promotes growth.

Key Principle 2:
Trustworthiness and Transparency

Transparency in a relationship can help facilitate trust. Sometimes people think that being transparent means telling all of your secrets, but that's not true. Transparency means to be real, not fake. It means to be honest about your motives and plans. It starts with treating the church more like a gathering of people than a performance. I have been a part of a large church for over 20 years. The lead staff on stage seems to forget that not everyone knows who they are and how the church functions. Simply introducing yourself on stage and telling everyone your role, acknowledging that there may be some new people in the audience, can be helpful. Also in plain language, stating why we do the things we do may help.

If you're a pastor, preaching from your own experience and openly acknowledging your weaknesses and hurt can go a long way in building trust. It shouldn't be a confessional; that's not the purpose of preaching. Its purpose is to share the Gospel, the Good News of Christ. Yet, if we the listeners can't see why you would need it in your life, why should we need it in ours? Trauma survivors want to know that church leaders understand and have experienced pain like theirs. They want to know that they will be treated with respect and that they'll fit in with the other people, rather than stand out because no one here has ever had anything like that happen to them. It doesn't have to be the same kind of wounding. But as a leader, I know that if I don't go out of my way to share my brokenness, the people I'm leading think I've got it all together and somehow have a perfect life. That is so far from the truth! I'm entirely aware of all the mistakes I've made with my children, staff, spouse, and friends, even as I write this. Many times, I've broken trust with the people in my life. When that happens, most often, an acknowledgment and a request for forgiveness go a long way. Most people are willing to forgive and move forward when we make mistakes. As a leader, sometimes watching you handle an error humbly and sincerely is the best thing for trust-building.

Key Principle 3: Peer Support

Offer opportunities to connect with other people with similar histories and desires. I think this has been both the advantage of the church and the struggle. As churches grow in number, it's been a challenge to connect people in small groups. There is quite a lot of study into cell groups, home groups, life groups, and other ways a church can organize itself. Schools are already organized by age and level of experience. Trauma survivors need an opportunity to connect with other trauma survivors while also having a safe environment to prevent further abuse. One thing we are trying to do at Trauma Education & Consultation Services, Inc., is to create a trauma-specific support group that churches can offer their members. Other peer support groups like Celebrate Recovery and Grief Share have successfully offered peer support, as long as they stay focused on their purpose. Small groups can provide opportunities for support in a way that large groups can't. We want to duplicate this success, but with a focus on the survivors of past trauma.

Key Principle 4: Collaboration and Mutuality

Collaboration and mutuality mean to have the attitude that we are all in this together. It is not me versus you or me fixing you; it is us healing together. I shared the story of how God first introduced me to trauma counseling in another book. When faced with a client saying she was "stuck," I agreed with her rather than try to change her feelings. I was honest that I, too, felt stuck. I practiced humility and transparency. Not that I'm such a good person, but I didn't know what else to do! Then, I practiced collaboration and mutuality. I told her, "God will show us what to do." We'll pray and see what He shows us; not me. We are all broken in some way, and that is the truth. Looking at my previous definition of trauma, we've all experienced something in our lives that has robbed us and impacted our identities. Indeed, we are all in this together. When we admit it and openly acknowledge it to each other, we can work together for healing.

Key Principle 5: Empowerment

Empowerment means putting the power for change in the hands of the survivor. We all have choices and have to exercise our right to make decisions. You can't force someone to accept Christ, though many have tried. You can't force someone to talk about their past trauma. Our approach is to educate them about the impact of trauma on their lives, and give them a choice, using a structured and strategic approach to heal from their wounds. The rest is really up to them. We, as leaders, can't take on the responsibility to heal people. God is the source of all healing, whether natural or miraculous. We can connect people to God's healing and facilitate that process by partnering with God. But we have to put the power of choice in the hands of the wounded survivor.

Key Principle 6:
Sensitivity to Cultural, Historical, and Gender Issues — Recognizing Generational and Historical Trauma

Generational and historical trauma refer to unique experiences. Generational trauma is trauma passed down from one generation to the next. My parents both had abusive, alcoholic fathers, and their fathers were also abusive. My parents made the decision to end the generational trauma, and they did. However, their sisters carried it on down to the next generation.

Historical trauma is an abuse on a mass scale that affects many people because of their skin color, country of origin, or other factors outside of their control. Like all trauma, it's cumulative, one building on the other and creating a massively traumatic experience for people groups, even if the events happened before their lifetime. This becomes embedded in their identity and continues to be built upon by their personal experiences.

In our current political climate, this may be one of the more controversial subjects. However, I believe it shouldn't be contentious in the Christian church. This is not about politics or who is right or wrong. Instead, it's about the person, the trauma survivor, sitting under your ministry. It's not about ideas; it's about people. John quoted Jesus, saying, "So now I am giving you a new commandment: Love each other. Just as I have loved you, you should love each other. Your love for one another will prove to the world that you are my disciples" (John 13: 34-35, NLT). Loving others means being sensitive to their experience and not judging by our own. America is still reeling from the impact of the Civil War and the legal practice of chattel slavery. The Holocaust and World War 2 still impact us, not to mention the more recent wars on terror.

Many African American people have ancestors who were brought to this country aboard slave ships. Slave owners dehumanized African people so they could justify their atrocious behavior. Unfortunately, mainline Christian denominations supported this, even teaching that it was God's will. Eventually, it was a smaller denomination that helped to end slavery in America. Some denominations have held conferences to apologize for their ancestors and try to make reparations. Slavery has ended, Jim Crow has ended, but there is still a disparity in how many communities treat people of color. Social media and the news tell horrific stories of mistreatment and abuse.

We cannot, for one minute, think this doesn't affect the people in our Christian groups, no matter their skin color. I happen to be a white female who grew up in a multi-cultural environment. My parents taught me that all people are equal and that we should value other ethnicities, not tolerate them. In the last church my father pastored in California, there were 13 different nationalities. In a church of approximately 150, this was pretty diverse. And, more than one person of color served in the leadership and on stage. I grew up thinking this was normal and how everyone lived. Later, when we moved to Kansas and then to Georgia, my experience changed. My Chinese friends in California had such colorful houses and rich heritage, and my Latina friends had such beautiful brown skin. I came to think being white was boring. When I was old enough to understand how badly people of color were treated, I was shocked and appalled. As a white person, unlike my friends, the difference was that I didn't have to think about my skin color every day.

Historical trauma doesn't affect Black people only, although that's what I've discussed the most, due to the current social environment. Others are impacted, too, including Indigenous, Native Americans, Jewish, Chinese, Japanese, Irish, Italian, Russian, and, because of 9/11, Americans in general. Not all individuals of the same ethnicity or race have the same experiences, however. We have to talk to the person, not the ethnicity. We must be sensitive to the person and their experiences, understanding that it might not be our experience, but accepting that it is theirs. This means asking questions about their lives, how they see God and the church, and why. It means being humble, open, and non-assuming.

As a female, I have also been subject to unfair and exclusionary experiences inside and outside Christian communities. My father told me I could be anything I wanted to be when I grew up. When I said I wanted to be a nurse, he said, "Be a doctor so you can be in charge!" I was heartbroken when I was old enough to understand that it wasn't true. Being sensitive to a woman's experience as opposed to a man's is also important, and vice versa. As I mentioned before, tracking sexual abuse statistics started as a feminist issue, and researchers didn't initially track the sexual abuse of boys. Men's sexuality is treated differently than girls' sexuality. Movies have been made that idolized the sexual abuse of boys by older women. Men and women are different. Their roles and experiences are different, and when we try to make them the same, it's like saying you're "color blind." Gender is an essential part of our identity and impacts our experiences, how we view the world, and how we view God.

Following the biblical mandates to love one another (John 13:34-35), put others above ourselves (Philippians 2), and not thinking of ourselves as more than we are (Galatians 6) can help us be more sensitive to others who are different than us. People aren't better or worse, just different. We are all sinners, and we all die and have to face God when it comes down to it. Jesus showed His disciples the proper way to relate to each other when He washed His disciples' feet.

He said we are to be servants to each other, not see ourselves as above each other. This sixth principle deals with serving and caring for others once we get politics and divisive talk out of the way.

One thing you, as a leader, could do is review the research and suggestions in *Where Do We Go From Here? How US Christians Feel About Racism and What they Believe it will Take to Move Forward,*" published by the Barna Group. This research was commissioned by The Reimagine Group of Alpharetta, Georgia. It's an ebook available exclusively through Barna, but you can get information at resources@barna.com. Discussing this amongst your leadership team, small group, or just with a friend could be helpful.

In 2017, the American Association of Christian Counselors released a documentary titled, *Unchained: Generational Trauma and Healing.* The film includes discussion questions, and this provides excellent opportunities for starting conversations with groups or individuals. The documentary can be found by a simple search on YouTube.com.

Another option is to take a personal race

inventory to help move your own story of race or ethnicity forward into your awareness, so you aren't acting on thoughts and beliefs lurking in the background. You can download a sample from my website, TraumaEducation.com/10reasons.html. After completing this inventory, you may share it with other leadership, group, or team members to increase your global awareness and make intentional decisions about your ministry group's racial issues.

These six principles can serve as a guide to implementing trauma-informed care at the third level of development. Perfection is unattainable, and you can't control other people's motives or thoughts. You can be intentional and continue to focus on the goals of increasing your community's trauma awareness. Before starting, you might rate yourself on a scale of 1-10. Say you see yourself as a 3. Then, chose a goal within a time frame. Maybe you want to get to 7 or 8 in two years. Intentionally moving forward will show your commitment to traumatized people in your group.

Level 4

Level 4 in the development of trauma-informed care is to become a trauma expert, choosing, learning, and practicing a trauma treatment model. Of course, I prefer my model, but many counselors learn different models and use them according to the client's preference. For counselors, there are now many options. Churches, schools, and small group leaders can find local counselors who do trauma work, are Christian-integrated and refer when needed. A church can become a trauma recovery hub by setting up a *Break EVERY Stinking Chain!: Healing for Hidden Wounds* class, small group or support group. At Trauma Education & Consultation Services, Inc., we consult with churches, Christian schools and other Christian organizations to help them institute the principles and set up systems to increase their care for people wounded by trauma.

As a pastor or pastoral counselor, you can also learn and institute this model. There are two significant mistakes that counselors make pertaining to trauma treatment. The first, and most common, is not asking about it. Most counselors focus on symptoms. It's a common mistake because behaviors are frequently visible while memories are not. People can tell you they feel depressed, aren't sleeping, struggle with anxiety, etc. But they don't always connect their current behavior to something that happened 20, 30 or even 40 years ago. The first myth I address in *Break EVERY Stinking Chain!: Healing for Hidden Wounds* is, "If it happened when I was a child, it doesn't affect me anymore."

As a ministry leader, people frequently come to you to discuss their issues. When it's appropriate, you can ask questions to determine if you need to make a referral. They should be thoughtful questions like, "Has anything happened to you that might be causing this pain in your life right now?" or maybe, "Is there anything you want to tell me that you'd like for me to know about your past or current life situation?" In some cases, you may ask, "Have you had any experiences of trauma in your childhood?" These questions show you have adopted the attitude of, "What's happened to you?" rather than, "What's wrong with you?"

Helping people through recently experienced painful or traumatic events is a common practice for ministry leaders. Having a format to follow can be helpful. Confidentiality is of utmost importance, of course, and the confessional rules bind senior pastors in most cases. Other ministry leaders aren't protected and must report any abuse to children under 18. That means you must be familiar with laws about reporting child abuse and have a plan in place just in case someone tells you about it.

For those more experienced, there are some handouts available in the workbook of *Break EVERY Stinking Chain! Workbook: Healing for Hidden Wounds* that can be helpful. These include the ACE Assessment, the Simple Trauma Source Assessment, and the Trauma Impact Handout. These should be used for discussion and education only. Then, if there is trauma present, refer the person to a trusted trauma-informed counselor. If you are not a trained counselor, please do not try to counsel trauma survivors! You need to know when to refer, after affirming their experience, normalizing it and assuring them that there is hope for healing.

The second mistake counselors make is pushing for details of the traumatic experience too soon before establishing a safe, emotionally secure relationship. This is where ministry leaders, pastors, teachers, and others have an advantage. When a person comes to a counselor, it's usually someone they don't know. People are more likely to disclose past trauma to someone they already trust and believe will treat them kindly. Sometimes they insist on sharing the details when their friend or pastor doesn't know what to do with the information. Don't push, but don't refuse to listen. Hearing horrific stories of abuse is difficult and can be traumatizing, especially if it's someone you are close to. Again, the best thing to do is refer to a counselor experienced in treating trauma survivors.

I have designed the Strategic Trauma & Abuse Recovery System to give counselors and clients a road map to follow. It's divided into three phases; I've broken down each phase into stages. You can read more about this in the training manual available on Amazon.com, The Strategic Trauma & Abuse Recovery System: A Christian-Integrated, Comprehensive, 3-Phase Model for Individual and Group Counseling. Counselors can get certified in this model, and so can churches. Instructions are available on our website at TraumaEducation.com. My vision is to see churches hosting a trauma support group for the first phase of recovery, and then referring to trained professional or experienced counselors for the second phase. For the third phase, I hope to see survivors returning to the support group as leaders and mentors, sharing what they've learned from the healing God has given them. This will bring together the church, experienced counselors, and the community to experience and promote healing from trauma.

Conclusion

I HOPE THIS LITTLE book has been helpful to you. I hope you have learned something new and gained some ideas to implement in your setting or ministry. Hopefully, we are constantly learning, growing, and listening to the Holy Spirit as He guides and transforms us. Because of that, this program is always going to be growing, changing, and improving! Please consider joining us on the journey to see people everywhere breaking the generational cycle of trauma and allowing God to heal their wounds.

Visit www.TraumaEducation.com to sign up for our email list and register for an upcoming training today.

Leave me a positive review on Amazon.com so that others will be drawn to this mission and vision, seeing God break the generational cycle of trauma in people's lives everywhere!

References

Anda RF, Felitti VJ, Walker J, Whitfield, CL, Bremner JD, Perry BD, Dube SR, Giles WH. (2006). The enduring effects of abuse and related adverse experiences in childhood: A convergence of evidence from neurobiology and epidemiology. European Archives of Psychiatry and Clinical Neurosciences; 256(3):174–86

Anda RF, Dong M, Brown DW, Felitti VJ, Giles WH, Perry GS, Edwards VJ, Dube SR. (2009). The relationship of adverse childhood experiences to a history of premature death of family members BMC Public Health;9:106.

Beck, R., & McDonald, A. (2004). Attachment to God: The Attachment to God Inventory, tests of working model correspondence, and an exploration of faith group differences. Journal of Psychology & Theology, 32(2), p. 92-103.

Benson, P., Donahue, M., & Erickson, J. (1989). Adolescence and religion: A review of the literature from 1970 to 1986. In D. O. Moberg & M. L. Lynn (Eds.), Research in the social scientific study of religion. Vol. 1, (pp. 153-181). Greenwich, CT: JAI Press.

Brokaw, B. F., & Edwards, K. J. (1994). The relationship of God image to level of object relations development. Journal of Psychology and Theology. 22, 352-371

Centers for Disease Control (CDC). 2021 found at https://www.cdc.gov/violenceprevention/aces/index.html?CDC_AA_refVal=https%3A%2F%2Fwww.cdc.gov%2Fviolenceprevention%2Facestudy%2Findex.html

Colson, R. D. (2012). Toward a more comprehensive, Biblically-integrated, theory and treatment of PTSD, substance abuse, and other trauma related disorders. A doctoral dissertation submitted to the Dean, Faculty of Christian Counseling and Spiritual Direction, International University for Graduate Studies.

Cusack KJ, Frueh BC, Hiers TG, et al. (2003). Trauma within the psychiatric setting: a preliminary empirical report. Administration and Policy in Mental Health 30:453–460,2003Crossref, Medline, Google Scholar

Dong M, Giles WH, Felitti VJ, Dube, SR, Williams JE, Chapman DP, Anda RF. (2004). Insights into causal pathways for ischemic heart disease: Adverse Childhood Experiences. Circulation; 110:1761–1766.

Dube SR, Felitti VJ, Dong M, Giles WH, Anda RF. (2003). The impact of adverse childhood experiences on health problems: evidence from four birth cohorts dating back to 1900. Preventive Medicine;37(3):268–277.

Ellis, A. (2000). Can rational emotive behavior therapy (REBT) be effectively used with people who have devout beliefs in God and religion? Professional Psychology: Research and Practice, Vol 31(1), 29-33.

Eurelings-Bontekoe, E. H. M., Hekman-Van Steeg, J., & Verschuur, M. J. (2005). The association between personality, attachment, psychological distress, church denomination and the God concept among a non-clinical sample. Mental Health, Religion & Culture, 8(2), 141-154.

Felitti, V. J., Anda, R. F., & Nordenberg, D., Williamson, D. F., Spitz, A. M., Edwards, V., Koss, M.P., & Marks, J.S., (1998). Relationship of childhood abuse and household dysfunction to many of the leading causes of death in adults: The adverse childhood experiences (ACE) study. American Journal of Preventive Medicine, 14(4), 245-258. Retrieved from http://download.journals.elsevierhealth.com/pdfs/journals/0749-3797/PIIS0749379798000178.pdf

Felitti, V. J. (2000). Videos. Cavalcade Productions, Inc.. Retrieved from http://www.cavalcadeproductions.com/ace-study.html

Felitti, V. J. (2004). The origins of addiction: Evidence from the Adverse Childhood Experiences study.

Goodman, S. H., & Gotlib, I. H. (1999). Risk for psychopathology in the children of depressed mothers: A developmental model for understanding mechanisms of transmission. Psychological Review, 106(3), 458–490. https://doi.org/10.1037/0033-295X.106.3.458

Harvard University: Center on the Developing Child. (N.D.). InBrief: The impact of early adversity on children's development (video). Retrieved from: http://developingchild.harvard.edu/resources/multimedia/videos/inbrief_series/inbrief_impact_of_adversity/

Institute for Family Studies. (2021) Retrieved from https://ifstudies.org/blog/the-us-divorce-rate-has-hit-a-50-year-low

Lifeway Research Report. (2014). Acute Mental Illness and Christianity [Internet]. Available from: https://lifewayresearch.com/wp-content/uploads/2014/09/Acute-Mental-Illness-and-Christian-Faith-Research-Report-1.pdf

Mental Health America (2021) Retrieved from https://www.mhanational.org/mentalhealthfacts

Mueser, K. T., Goodman, L. B., Trumbetta, S. L., Rosenberg, S. D., Osher, F. C., Vidaver, R., Auciello, P., & Foy, D. W. (1998). Trauma and posttraumatic stress disorder in severe mental illness. Journal of Consulting and Clinical Psychology, 66(3), 493–499. https://doi.org/10.1037/0022-006X.66.3.493

Mol, S., S., L, Arntz, A., Metsemakers, J., F., M., Dinant, G-J, Vilters-Van Montfort, P., A., P., and Knottnerus, J., A. (2005). Symptoms of post-traumatic stress disorder after non-traumatic events: Evidence from an open population study. The British Journal of Psychiatry, 2005; 186: 494 - 499.

National Association for Mental NAMI. (n.d.). Retrieved October 26, 2018, from https://www.nami.org/learn-more/mental-health-by-the-numbers

National Institute for Mental Health (n.d.) Retrieved from https://www.nimh.nih.gov/health/publications

NLT (The New Living Translation). (2004). The Holy Bible New Living Translation. Carol Stream, IL. Tyndale House Publishers.

Olff, M., Koeter, M., W., J., E. Van Haaften, H., Kersten, P., H., and Gersons, B., P., R., (2005). Impact of a foot and mouth disease crisis on post-traumatic stress symptoms in farmers. The British Journal of Psychiatry, 186: 165 - 166.

Our World in Datat (n.d.). Retrieved from https://ourworldindata.org/mental-health

Poole, J.C., Dobson, K.S., Pusch, D. (2017). Childhood adversity and adult depression: The protective role of psychological resilience, Child Abuse & Neglect, Volume 64, Pages 89-100. https://doi.org/10.1016/j.chiabu.2016.12.012.

Reinert, D. F., & Edwards, C. E. (2009). Attachment theory, childhood mistreatment, and religiosity. Psychology of Religion and Spirituality, 1(1), 25-34. Retrieved from http://ehis.ebscohost.com/ehost/pdfviewer/pdfviewer?vid=2&hid=116&sid=750ba4ff-09b4-4990-8cbf-4e4ee498460f%40sessionmgr110

Scott, M. J., and Stradling, S. G. (1994) Post-traumatic stress disorder without the trauma. Brit J Clin Psychol; 33: 71–4.

Shepherds Watchmen. Retrieved from https://shepherdswatchmen.com/browse-all-posts/why-pastors-leave-the-ministry/

van der Kolk, B. A. (January 1998). Psychology and psychobiology of childhood trauma. Prax Kinderpsychol Kinderpsychiatr. Vol. 47(1), pp. 19-35.

Wilkinson & Finkbeiner Attorneys. Statistics on divorce from various sources. Retrieved from https://www.wf-lawyers.com/divorce-statistics-and-facts/

Printed in Great Britain
by Amazon